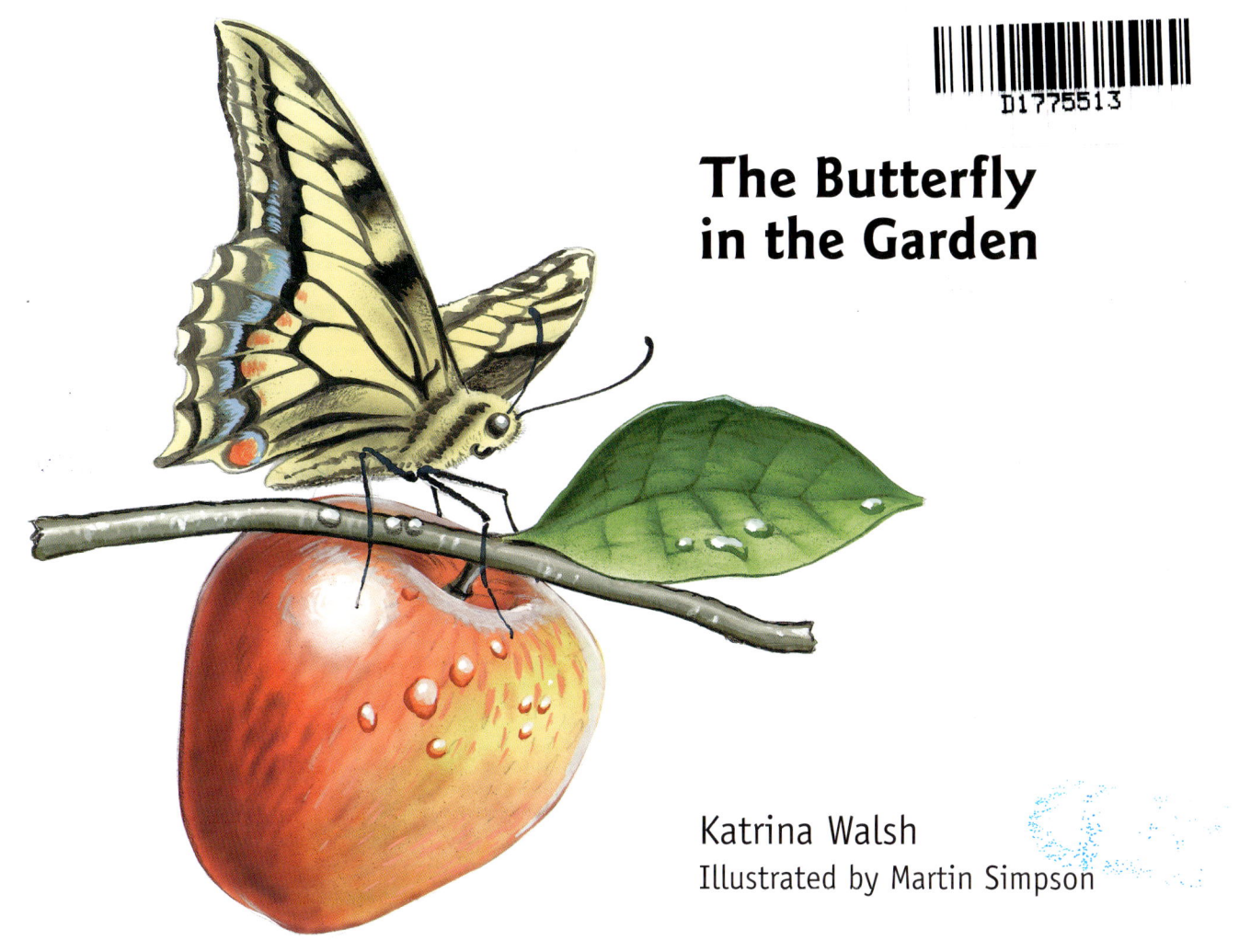

The Butterfly in the Garden

Katrina Walsh
Illustrated by Martin Simpson

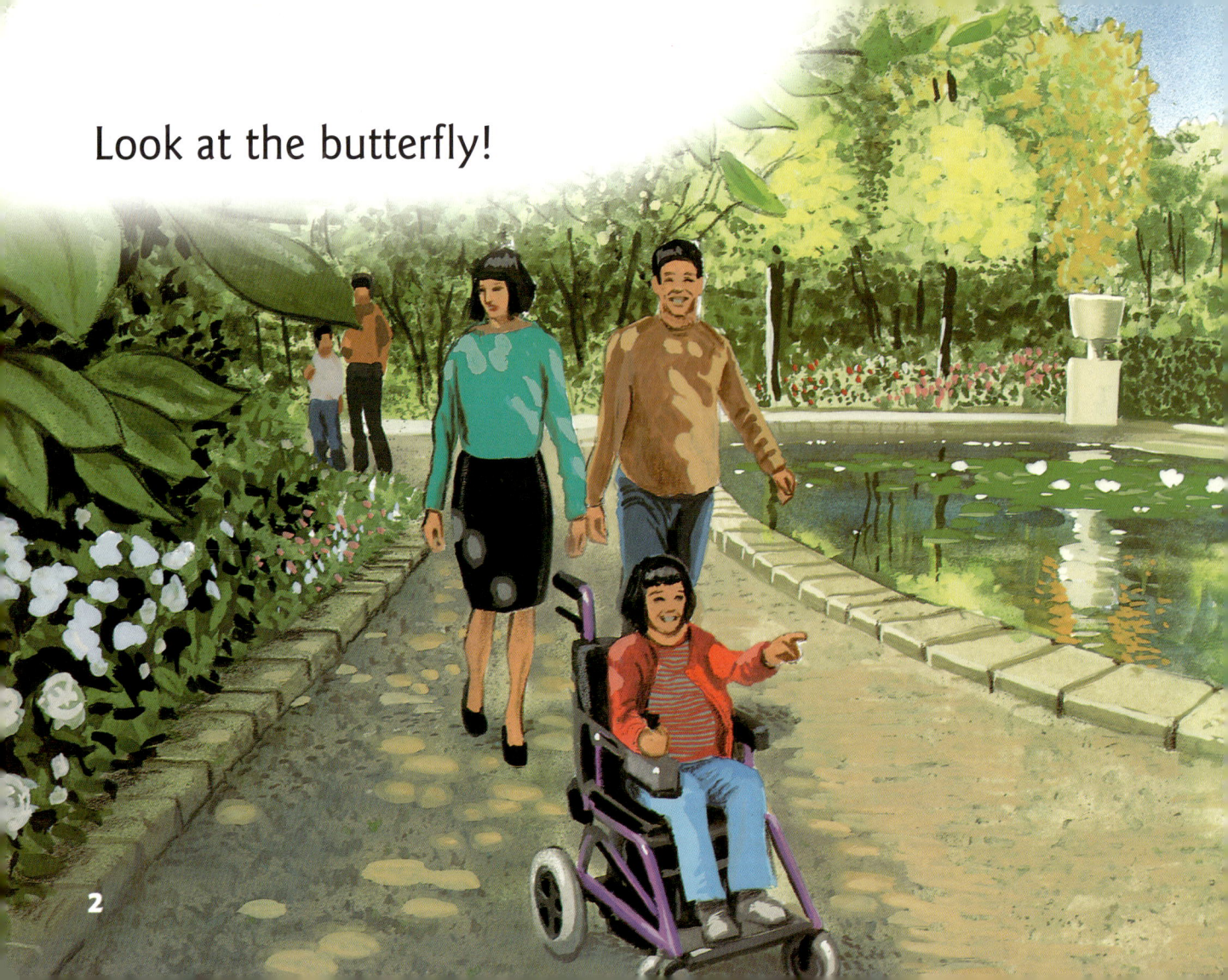

Look at the butterfly!

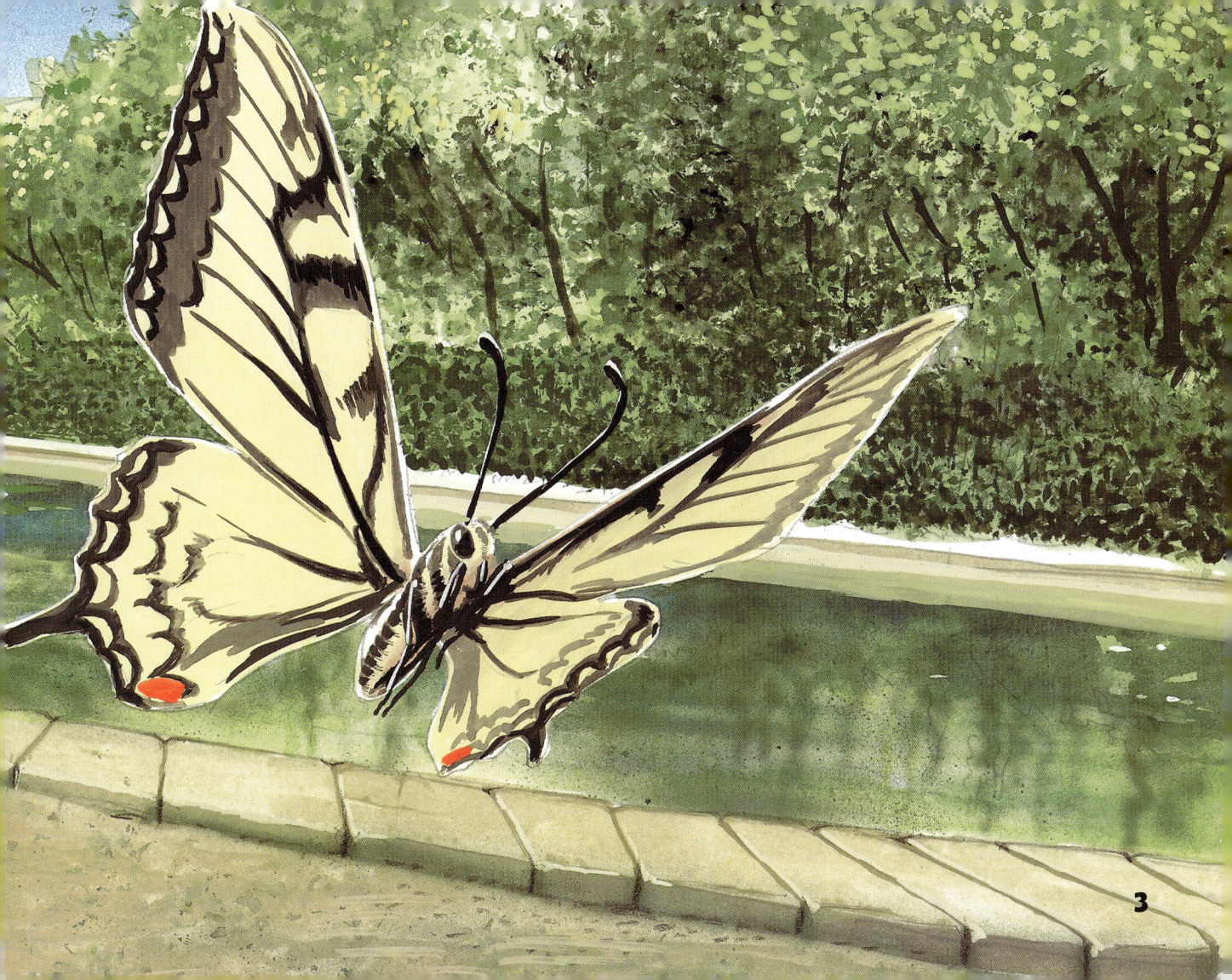

It is on the branch.

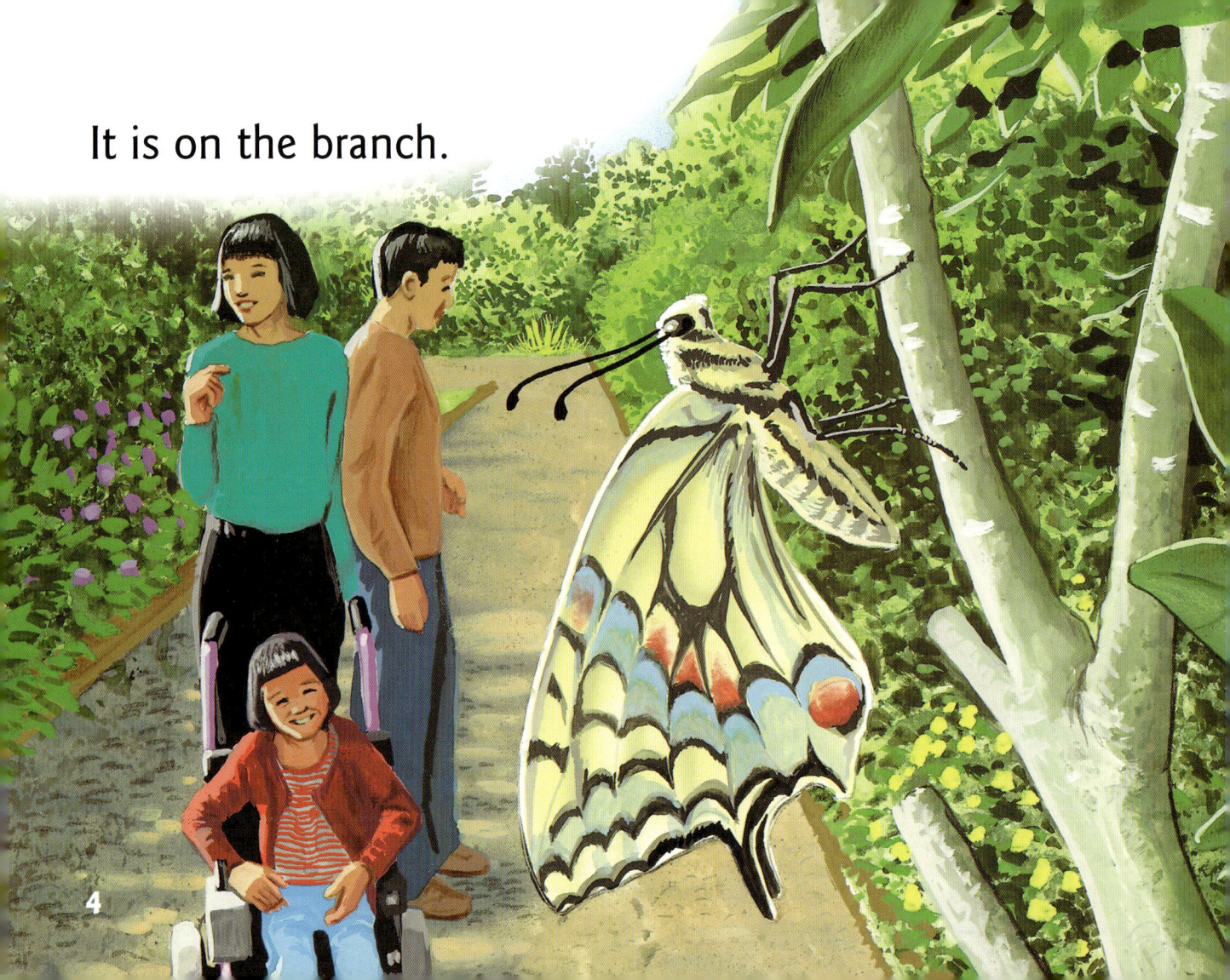

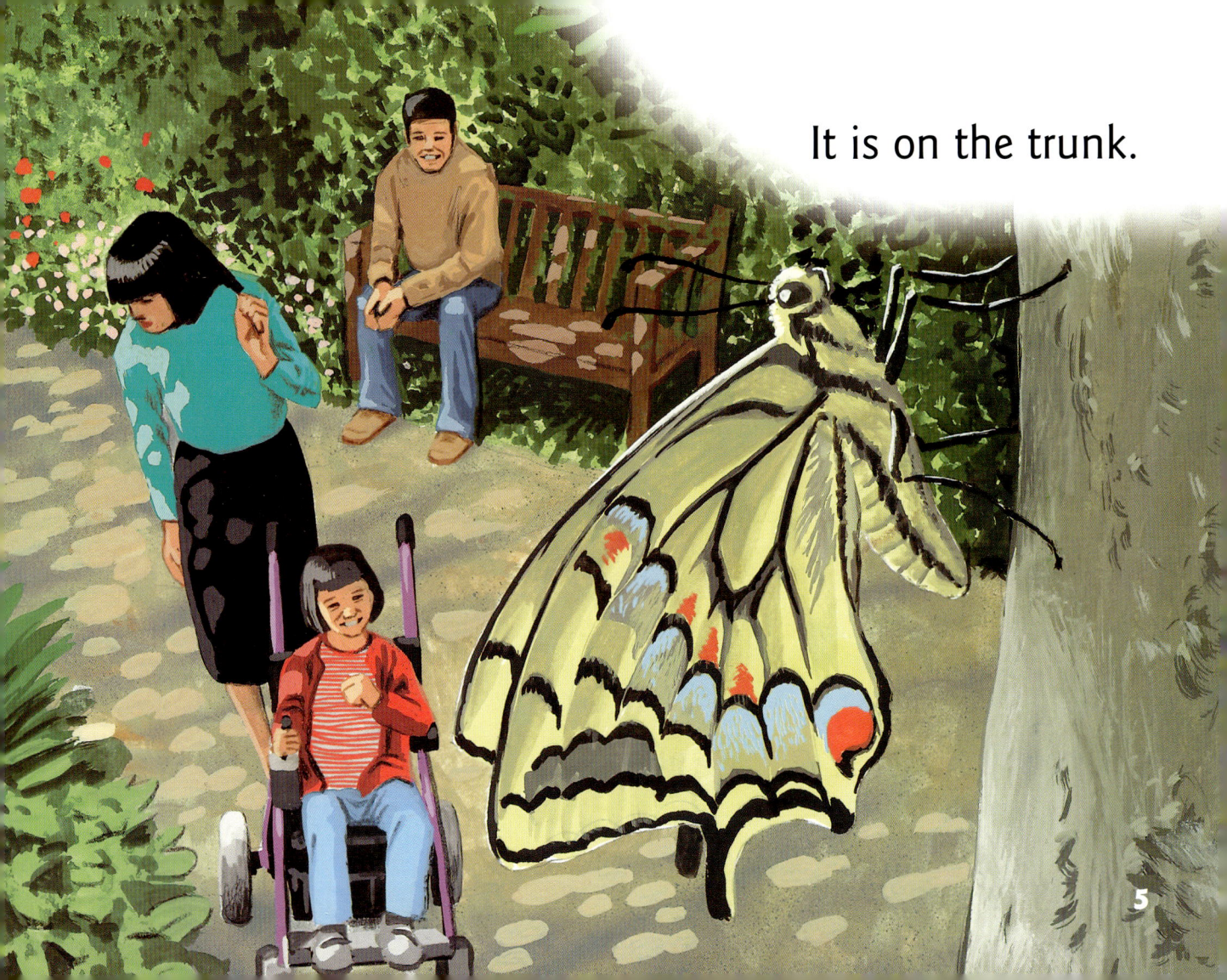
It is on the trunk.

It is on the apple.

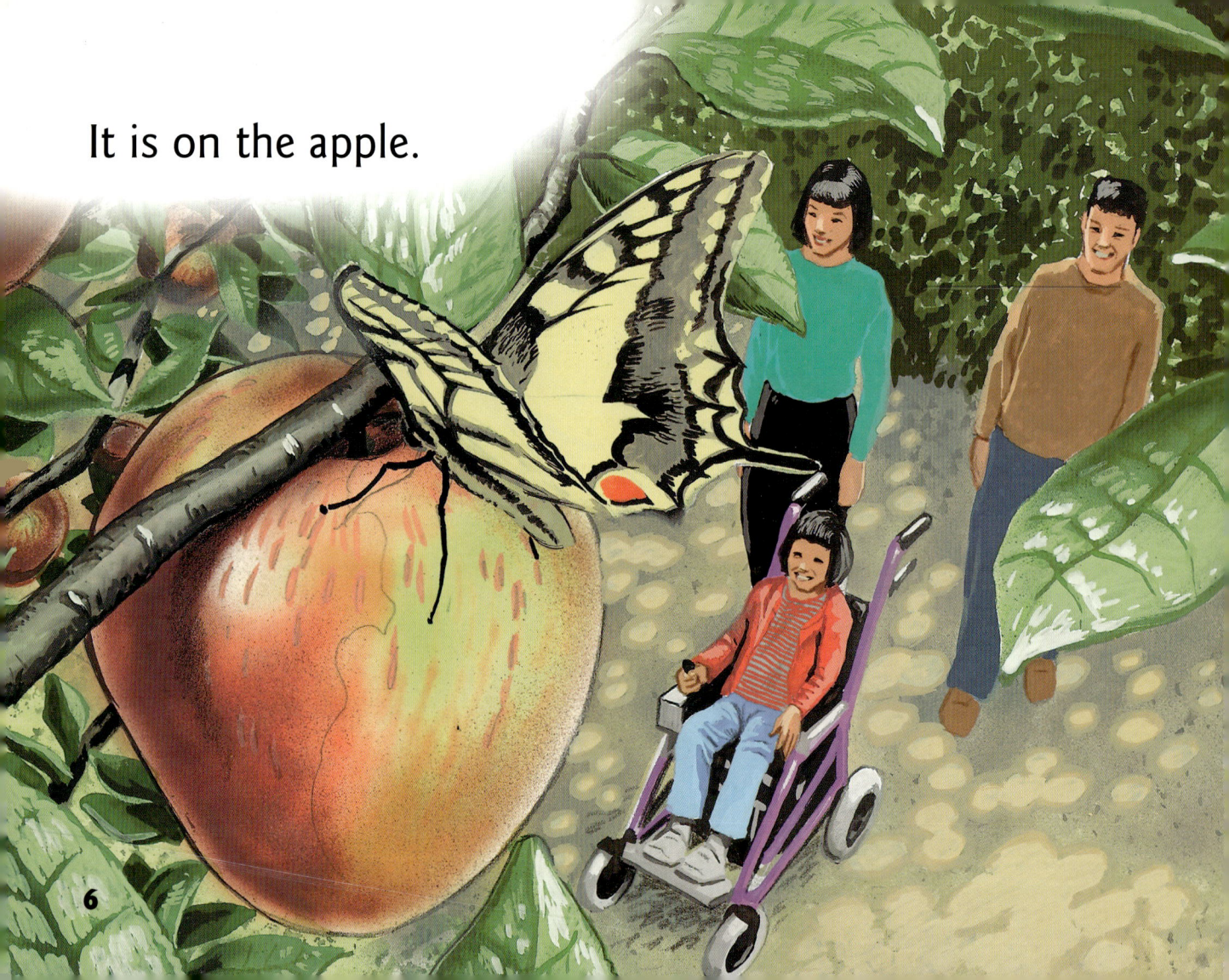

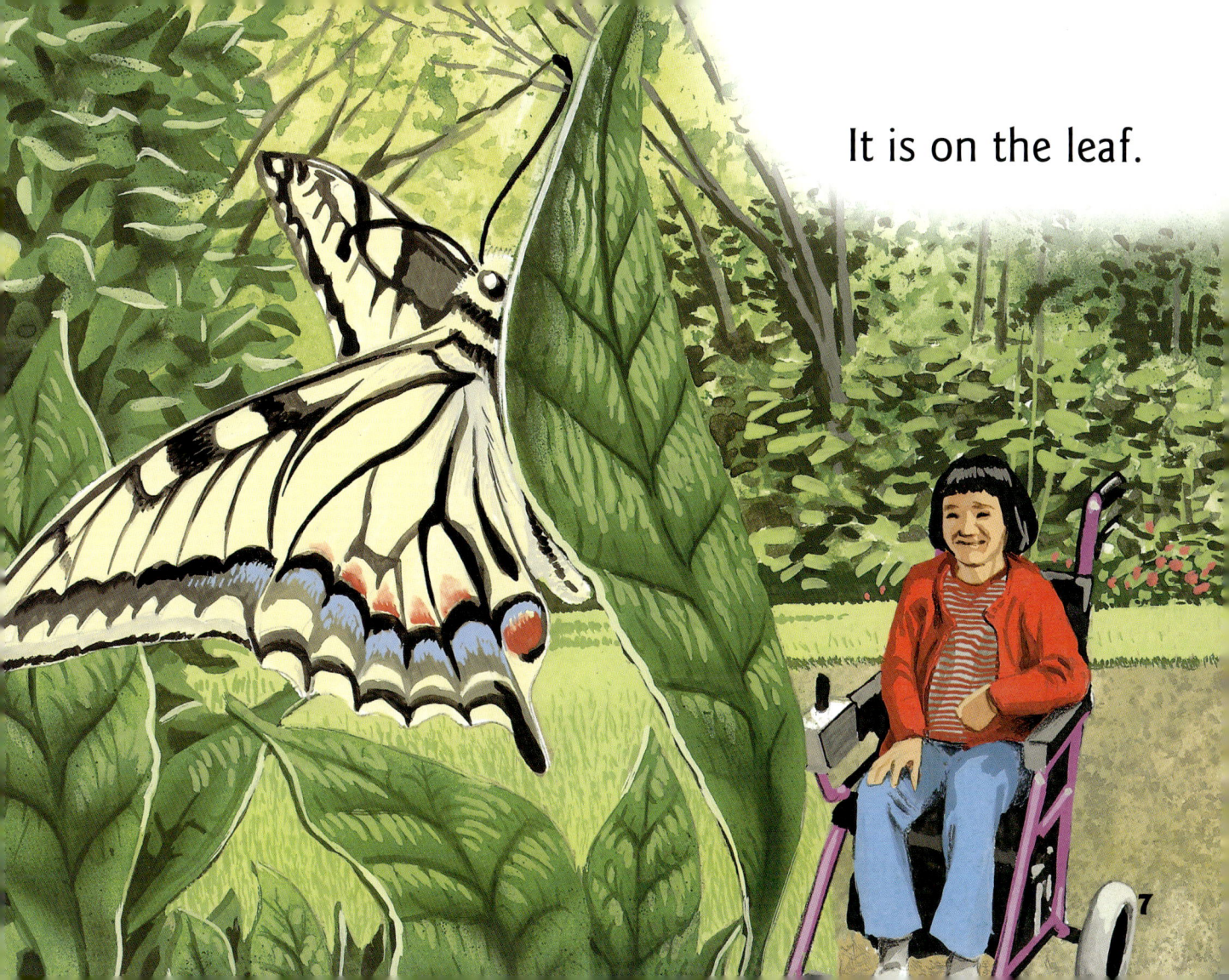

It is on the leaf.

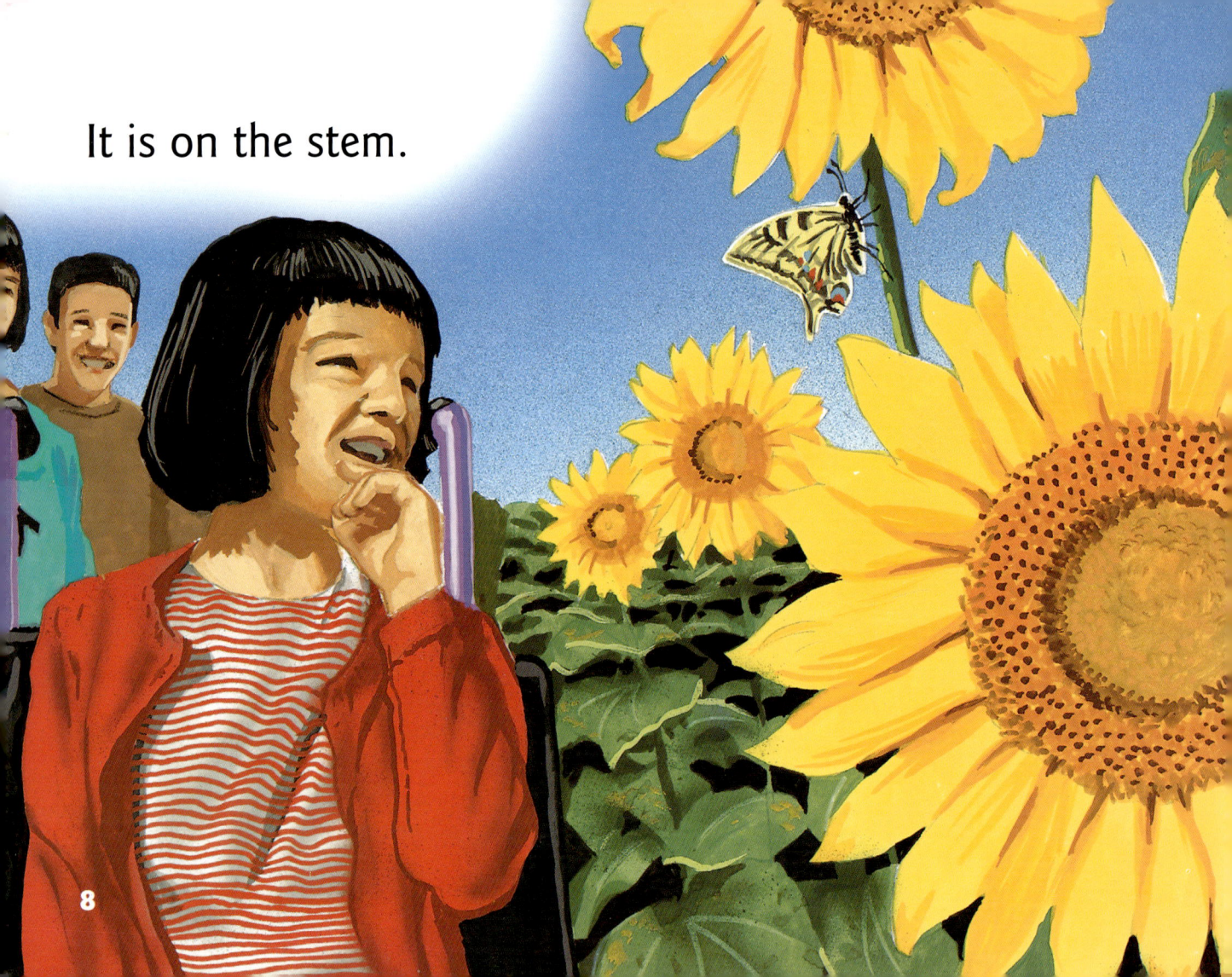

It is on the stem.

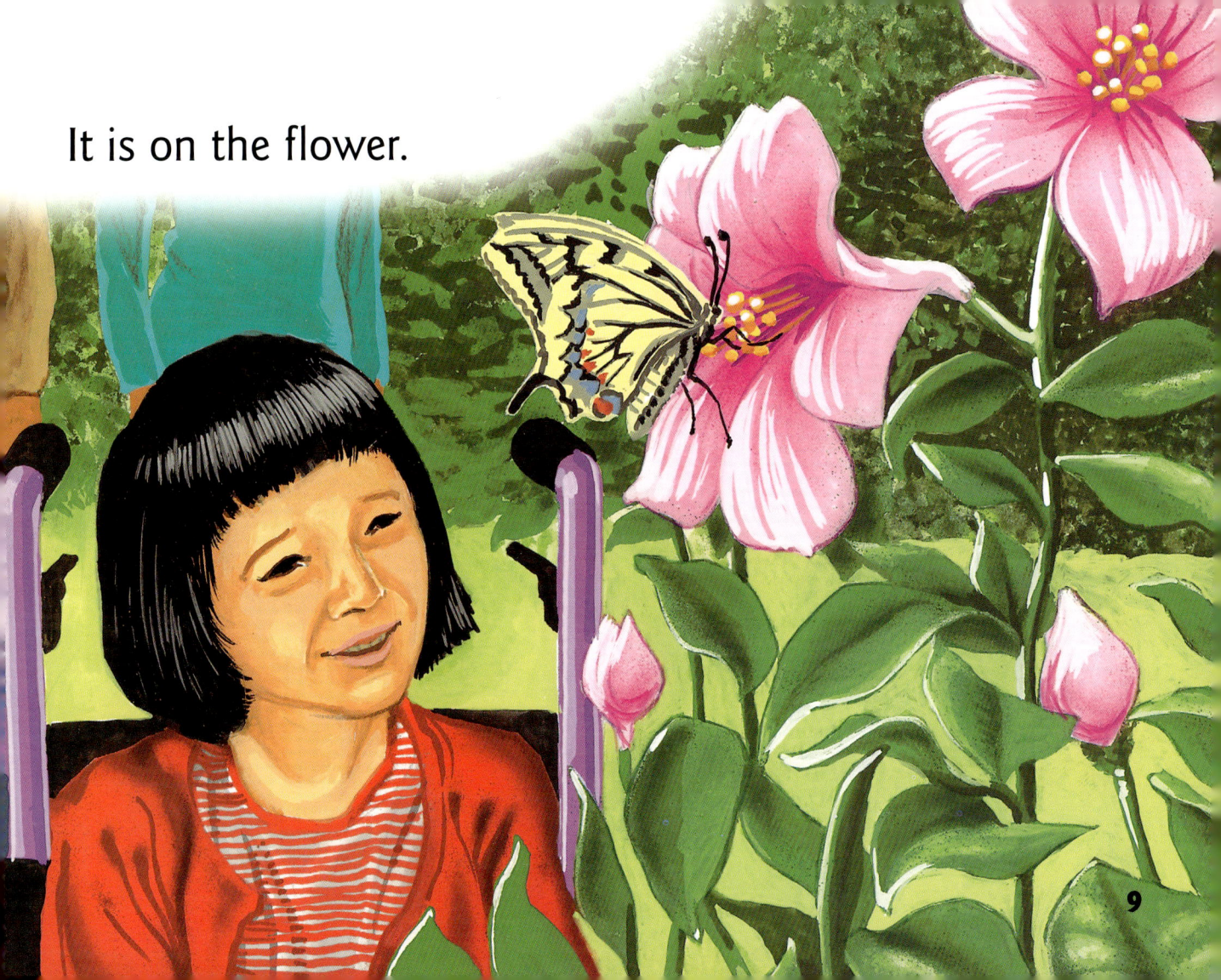

It is on the flower.

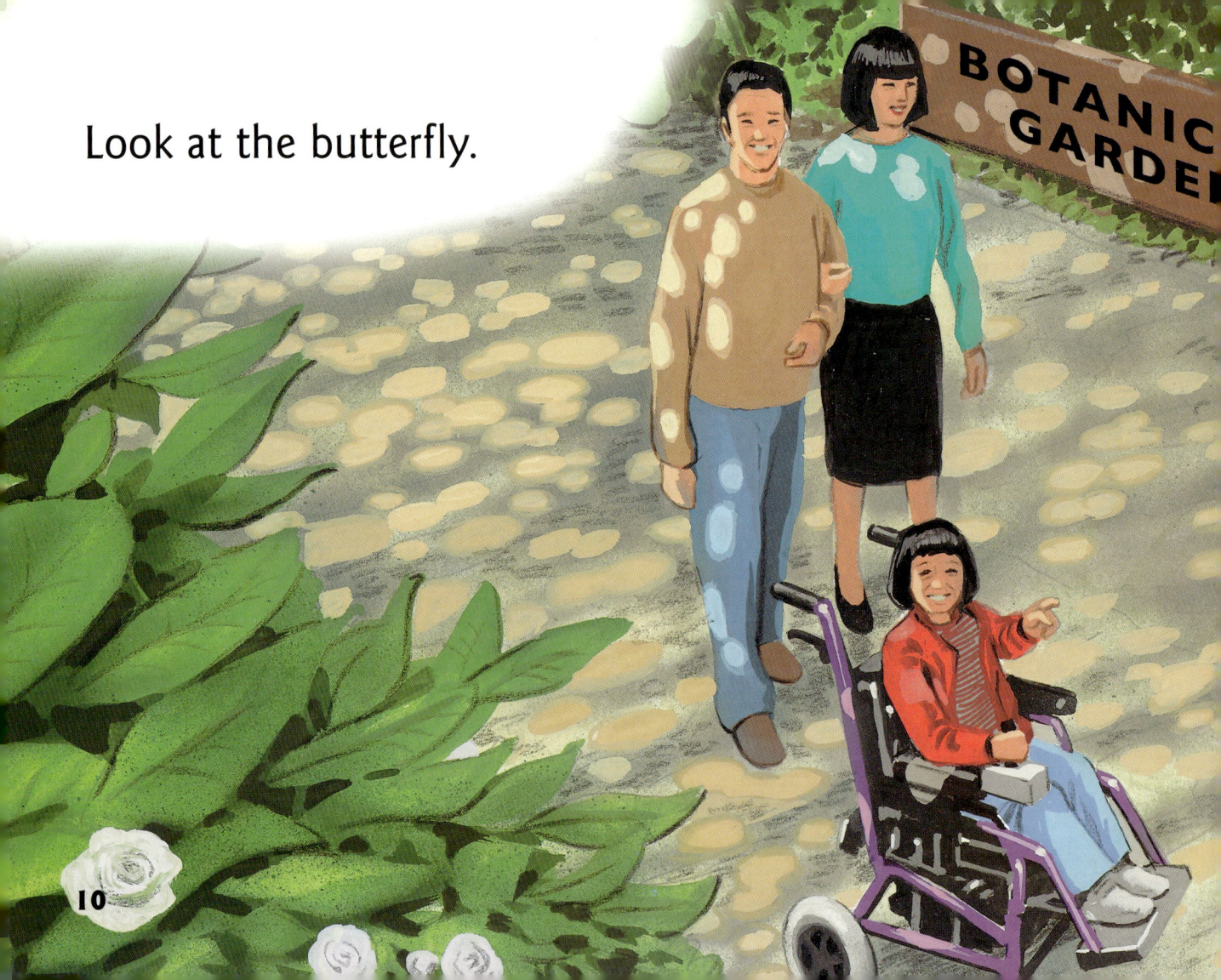

Look at the butterfly.

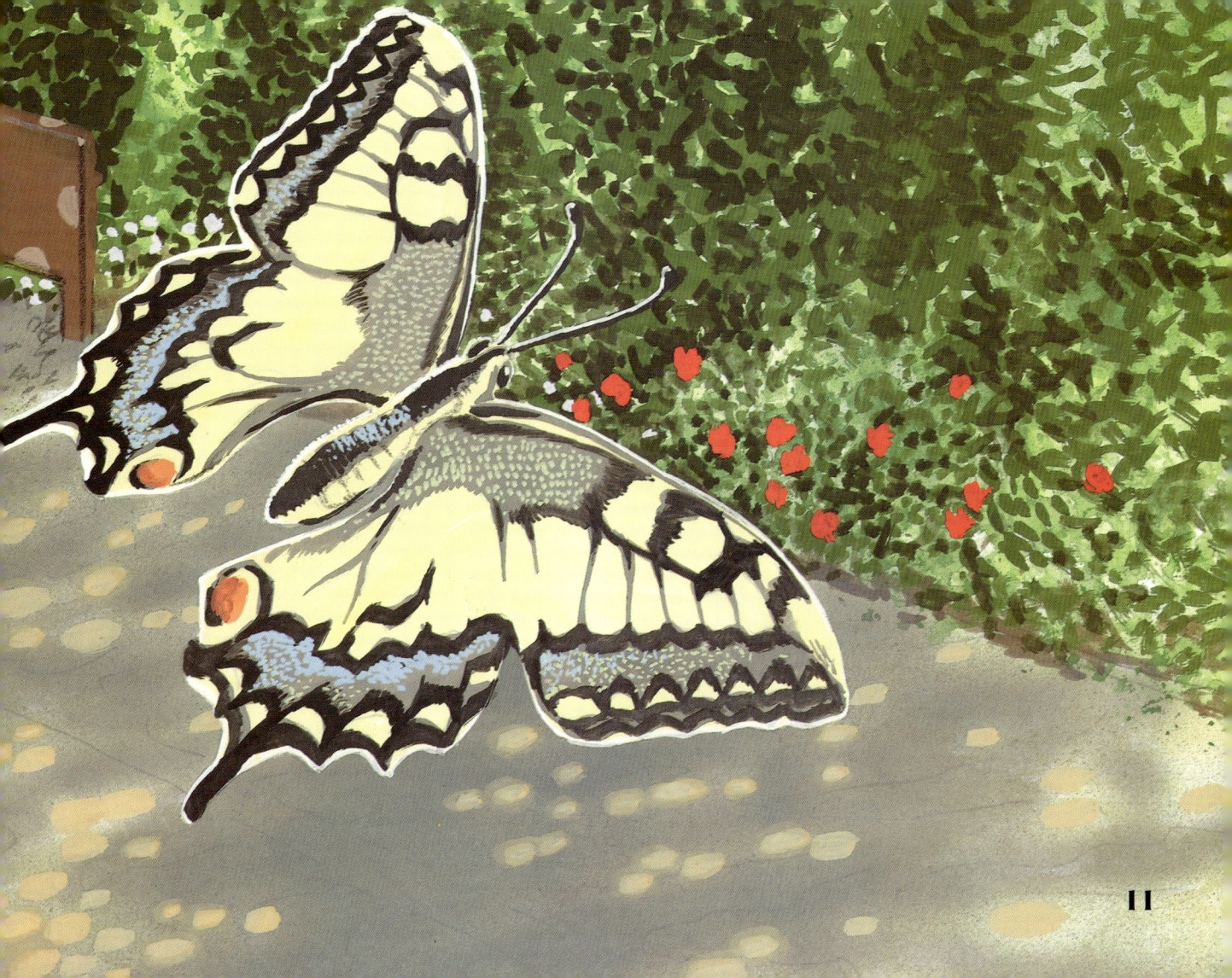

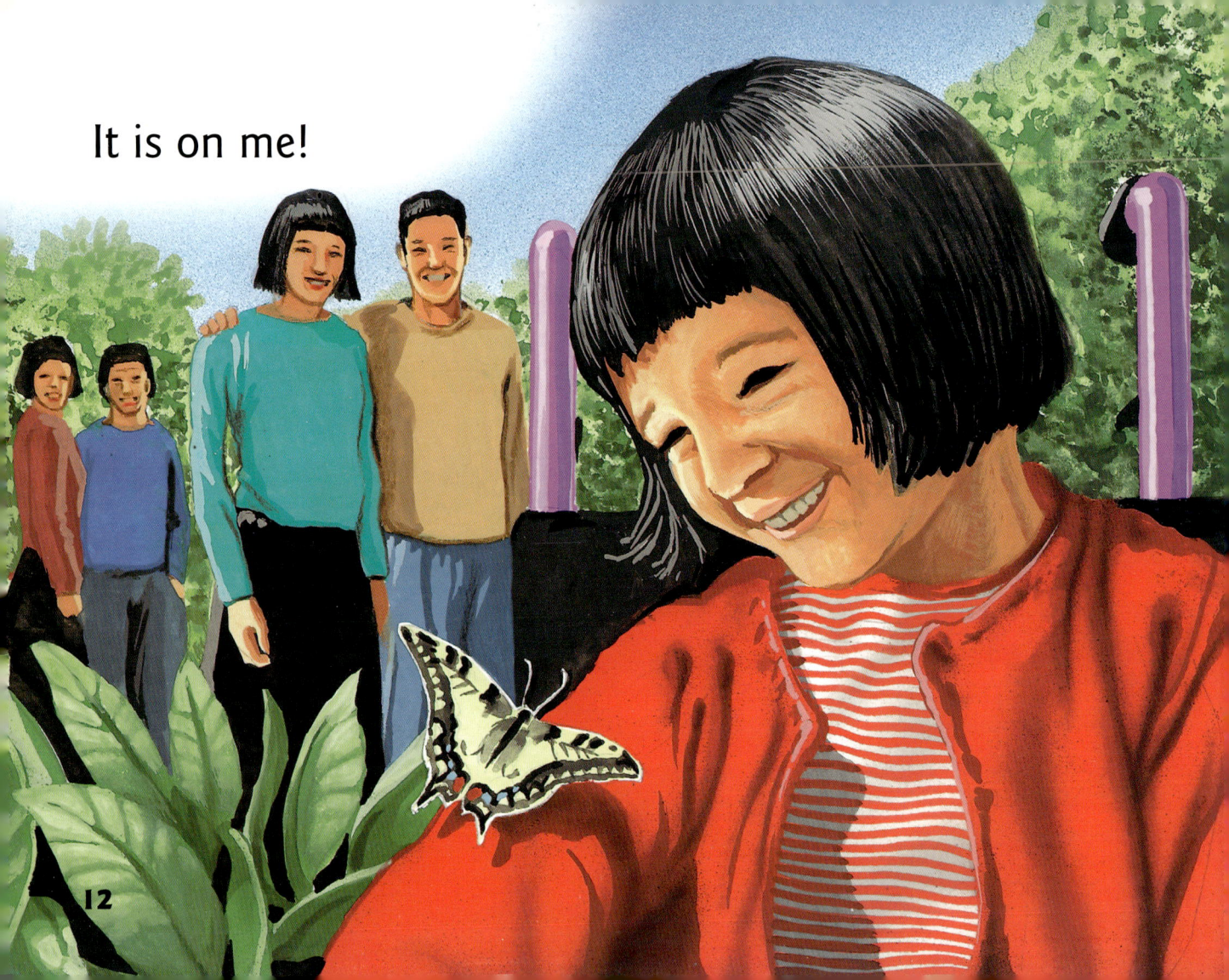